AN MGA ASUWANG: A BICOL BELIEF

By Francis X. Lynch, S.J

Reprinted 2019
The Philippine Social Sciences
and Humanities Review
Vol. XIV, No. 4,
pp. 401-427, December 1949

Contents

AN MGA ASUWANG: A BICOL BELIEF

Francis X. Lynch S. J.[*]

Introduction. Stories and beliefs about witches and witchcraft can be found in every part of the world. Almost every country can claim a generous share of them, and the Philippines is no exception. Here we possess our own traditional ideas on the subject, handed down through countless generations from our ancestors, and still very much alive today. In this paper the writer intends to set down beliefs of this sort which are current in one part of the Philippines, the Bicol region.

It was by chance that the writer first heard of the *asuwáng*. Subsequent inquiries during two years in the Bicol region revealed the existence of a very interesting if somewhat complex group of beliefs and half-beliefs concerning this witchlike class of human beings which, in Bicol, are designated *an mga asuwáng*.

In the Bicol region — as throughout most of the Philippine lowlands — belief in the *asuwáng* is a living belief. It is a belief kept alive by the stories told the children by their parents and grandparents; by the traditional explanations of a scratching on the roof by night, a shadow flitting across the near-full moon, or

[*] Obtained his M.A., 1949; Department of Anthropology and Sociology, University of the Philippines.—*Editor.*

the cry of the bird of ill omen. *Asuwáng* stories are dismissed as nonsense by a few, doubted as unproved by many, accepted as true by most. Whether the belief is justified or not, it is there. In the following pages will be found an attempt to synthesize the content of that belief as it exists in the principal towns of the provinces of Camarines Sur and Albay.[1]

Meaning of the generic term asuwáng.[2] The term *asuwáng* is known and used throughout the entire Bicol region as the name for a person male or female) who practices witchcraft.[3] More accurately, an *asuwáng* is understood a man or woman possessing preternatural powers of locomotion and

---

[1] The sources of the material contained herein are (1) notes made front personal observation and inquiry during a stay of two years (1946-48) in the Bicol region of southeastern Luzon, and (2) the reports of fifty-seven Ateneo de Naga college students who were trained as investigators in this particular subject and carried out their field work in April 1948. For the local distribution of their reports and informants, see Appendix II.
Although a comparative study is outside the scope of the present paper, the writer has included, as Appendix III, some excerpts from Castaño's *Nòticia del Bicol.* Fr. Castaño describes the *asuwáng* belief as it existed at the coming of the Spaniards — markedly different from the present-day tradition.

[2] Throughout this paper the author uses the orthography of the National Language Institute, as applied to Bicol. Proper place names are spelled according to the *Gazetteer of the Philippine Islands* (Washington, D.C.: Coast and Geodetic Survey, 1945).

[3] Unfortunately, the English word "witch" has come to be used for females only; hence the local term, *asuwáng*, will be employed in this study.

metamorphosis and an inhuman appetite for the voided phlegm and sputum of the deathly sick, as well as the flesh and blood of the newly dead. These powers and appetites are acquired either by a pact, implicit or explicit, with the evil spirits, or by means of imitative magic, or by both.[4]

Such is the meaning of the word *asuwáng* in the Bicol region of today. The origin of the term is less clear, though it is probably derived from the word *áso,* meaning *dog.* Since the Bicol word for dog is not *áso* but *ayám,* there is an indication that the term was borrowed or introduced from another region, a point which is outside the scope of the present descriptive paper.

Two name-origin theories, offered by informants living in widely separated towns, are worthy of mention here. A man of Magarao, Camarines Sur, tells us that the word *asuwáng* is derived from "... *kaguwáng,* an animal of the fox type which has as its

---

[4] This definition was arrived at inductively and is, properly speaking, a conclusion of this study. It is given at this point for the more ready orientation of the reader.

By "imitative magic" is here understood that branch of sympathetic magic which is based upon the "law of Similarity" (See J. G. Frazer, *The Golden Bough* [New York: The Macmillan Co., 1942] 11ff.). In the present subject matter, note especially the causal nexus which is believed to exist between the *asuwáng's anting-anting* or charm, a chick, and his preternatural power of flight.

food fowls and other smaller animals."[5] Another informant, from a barrio of Aroroy on the island of Masbate, claims that *"Asuwáng* is derived from *ashô.* This is a kind of animal whose physical structure resembles that of the bear, for it has a long and protruding mouth which is provided with sharp canine teeth to enable it to suck the blood of its prey."[6] It is noteworthy that neither informant refers the term to the word *áso*, but both make reference to a carnivorous, long-snouted mammal.

Kinds of asuwáng. All *asuwáng* are alike in that they possess the basic qualities contained in the generic definition given above (pp. 2f). However, they may be divided into two species according to their mode of locomotion. This division should be accepted with reservation, for it appears that the same *asuwáng* may possess both powers, that of flight and that of swift walking.

Represented schematically, the species and sub-

---

[5] This derivation-theory is interesting, because in the islands to the south of the Bicol peninsula — Samar, Leyte, Bohol, Mindanao and Basilan — there is found a mammal called *kagumang*. Moreover, the *kaguwang (Galeopithercus volans* Shaw or *Galeopithecus philippinensis* Wath.) has the lateral skin folds which are, in modified fashion, ascribed to the *asuáwng*. See "Carta del P. Francisco de P. Sanchez al R.P. Rector del Ateneo," *Cartas de los Padres de la Campañia de Jesús de la Misión de Filipinas* 9 (1891) 147; also see *A Hand List of the Most Common Minerals, Plants and Animals in the Philippine Islands* (Manila: Ateneo de Manila, 1920) 178.

[6] For the meaning of *asbô* in certain parts of Camarines Sur and Albay, see below.

species of *asuwáng* would be as follows:

a s u w á n g

1.   *asuwáng na layóg* (walking *asuwáng)*
In some District this species is called *asbô.*

2.   *asuwáng na layóg* (flying *asuwáng*)
A special kind of *asuwáng na layóg* is called the *ananánggál* ("detached"), because in its flight only the head and internal organs take to the air while the trunk and limbs remain on the ground.

In the paragraphs which follow, each of the above mentioned kinds of *asuwáng* will be described briefly. Then the more generalized asuwáng-beliefs will be set down.

Asuwáng na lakáw. This kind of *asuwáng,* the walking species, is by far the more common. Informants are divided in their opinions as to the formulas and magic ointments used by these persons, but the nightly schedule of operations seems fairly well agreed upon. About six o'clock in the evening, when darkness has all but fully set in, the *asuwáng na lakáw* must decide where he (or she) will go that night. This the *asuwáng* determines in one of many ways, all of which presuppose a sense of hearing which is extremely acute. He may for instance, put his ear to the rice mortar and listen for the sounds of mourners; he may, according to some, listen for these sounds while standing on his head with his head in a shallow hole in the ground. Others say that the *asuwáng* has a well which is used just for this purpose; he merely removes the cover, drops into the opening and listens.

It is usually near eight o'clock when the *asuwáng na lakáw* leaves his home and goes off in the direction of the prey he has previously located. Some informants say that the walking *asuwang,* like the flying variety, apply some unknown but bad-smelling oil to their bodies, with the result that they can walk with the swiftness of the wind, weaving in and out of house-posts with the greatest of ease. Other informants maintain that this power of swift movement and the power of metamorphosis are *automatically* gained — or regained — with the coming of darkness.

The walking *asuwáng* may leave home in his own human form or may adopt that of an animal, if he believes the change expedient. According to one informant, he takes the form of the very first animal which he meets on the way, be it dog cat or pig, and in this guise proceeds to the house where his intended host is. The majority of informants, however, say that the choice of form is completely free.

Upon reaching the house of the sick person whom he seeks, the *asuwáng na lakáw,* if he has retained his human form, cautiously places himself under the house, beneath the mat or bed of the patient. Since the mat is on the split-bamboo floor, or the bed only slightly raised above the floor, and since the house floor is at least five feet above the ground, the *asuwáng* has no difficulty in taking up a position directly beneath the sick person. (At this point, the details become rather vivid.)

The *asuwáng* have a special preference for the tubercular who void a great amount of phlegm and blood. According to the informants, when such a person is sick, the split-bamboo flooring is opened a little so that he may expectorate more conveniently. Beneath such an opening the *asuwáng* attaches himself "like a hanging bat" and takes his food. If he is surprised in this activity, he may turn himself into a house-post or any one of innumerable swit-footed animals and so escape — unless his pursuers know the proper charms for capturing *asuwáng*.

Some informants speak of the satiated *asuwáng* as looking like a woman "eight months advanced in the family way." Further, it is said that this *asuwáng* has teats the size of full-ripened cherries, and it is this characteristic which makes it easy to pick out a man who is an *asuwáng*. Upon returning home after filling himself at a sick person's house, the *asuwáng* is said to nurse his children at the breast.

The *asuwáng* usually spends most of the night and predawn morning at the homes of the sick, dying or dead. The most common opinion is that he is back at his own by four o'clock in the morning. He either loses his preternatural powers with the first streaks of dawn or, according to some, bathes in the river to remove the magic oil he had previously applied and is thus restored jr his normal state.

There is another way in which the *asuwáng na lakáw* can visit his victim, and this is adopted especially when he wishes to "snatch a corpse" from under the very eyes of the gathered mourners. Rendering himself invisible, the *asuwáng* enters the room in which the wake is taking place. He then substitutes for the body a banana plant stalk and goes off with the corpse. The *asuwáng* is so clever, we are told, that his banana stalk substitute cannot be distinguished from the real thing, except by the former's "having no fingerprints."

In the Partido de Lagonoy, Pili, Rinconada and southern Albay districts, the designation *asuwáng na lakáw* is not used frequently as the alternate term *asbô*. The overwhelming majority of informants in these districts maintain that *asbô* and *asuwáng na lakáw* are synonymous, but there are some who consider *asbô* the equivalent of *asuwáng* in the generic sense. The word *asbô* is interesting, for in the minds of most it carries a derogatory connotation. Some believe it signifies "corpse-eater" or "man-eater" while others say that it means *asuwáng,* but in the scornful sense in which "mutt," for instance, is used of a nasty dog.

Asuwáng na layóg. There are two kinds of flying *asuwáng:* the simple *asuwáng na layóg,* and the *anananggál.* They differ in that the latter type leaves its trunk and limbs in some secluded spot while the head and entrails take to the air. The former flies with its entire body intact.

The flying *asuwáng* practice the same divinations as the *asuwáng na lakáw,* and they observe the same general schedule for operations; that is, from around eight in the evening till four in the morning.

Whereas in the case of the walking *asuwáng* there was some disagreement as to whether magic formulas and ointments were used, informants are unanimous in the belief that the flying *asuwáng* make use of both. The constituents of the flight-giving oil or ointment are disputed, but most are agreed that chicken dung plays a very important part. Some say that the solvent for the dung is coconut oil, while others add decayed human flesh and blood. This concoction is traditionally kept in a short bamboo tube one or two joints in length, although several informants make mention of a *tíbor,* or earthen jar.

When ready for his night flight, the flying *asuwáng* retires to some dark secluded spot, in his own home or in a deserted field. Dipping his right hand into the foul-smelling ointment which he has prepared, the *asuwáng* applies it in a line beginning from the tip of the little finger of his left hand, progressing the length of the arm to the armpit, thence down his left side and the outer side of his left leg, ending at the tip of the little toe. Then the left hand is dipped into the chicken-dung mixture and the process is duplicated on the right side of the body. During this operation, the *asuwáng* repeats to himself, but aloud, the following formula or its equivalent: *Sirí, sirí, dáing Diyós kung banggí; labáw sa ka-kahóyan, lagbás sa kasiróngan!* Literally translated, this formula reads

"Siri, siri, there is no God at night; over trees, under houses!" According to most informants, the repeated *siri* is for the onomatopoetic and rhyming effect, but the fact that it occurs again and again in such formulas seems to indicate that it has an added magical meaning.[7] The phrase *dáing Diyós kung banggí* is considered a denial of the power of God at night and, simultaneously but implicitly, the sealing of a pact with the evil spirits to gain the sought-for powers of flight. The petitioned powers are figures in the closing phrases: "over trees, under houses."

There are many other formulas, but the most common is *Fuéra Diyós, fuéra húlog* ("Away with God, away with falls".) In each such formula there is the double element of a pact with evil spirits and an expression of the flight-powers desired by the operator.

According to some informants, after the *asuwáng* has applied the ointment with the proper words, an oily membrane appears on both sides of the body similar to the lateral skin folds of the "flying lemur" (*Dermoptera*).[8] Others say that no membrane actually appears, but the power of flight is given without these "wings."

At this point, if the *asuwáng* is the ordinary *asuwáng*

---

[7] There is a Bicol verb *nagsisisiri* which means "to simmer" or "to sizzle," but no informant mentioned any connection between the *siri, siri* of the formula and this word.

[8] See note 5, above.

na layóg, he flaps his arms, jumps and hops about and then ascends into the night sky. He does not fly like a bird, but walks through the air at a swift pace. If, however, the *asuwáng* is an *anananggál,* he props himself against a house wall or, if he be in the open, against a secluded tree or river bank, and, like a cork from a bottle, his head detaches itself from the trunk and limbs. The head, with the *asuwáng's* internal organs attached, flies away into the night.

As the flying *asuwáng* races through the night, there is heard the cry *kakák* or *kikík.* Some informants say that this sound is made by the bird of ill omen which is the herald of the *asuwáng,* but most maintain that it is not this bird (the *báro-kikík)* that is heard. Rather, it is either the flier himself or the chick which resides in the stomach or innards of all *asuwáng.*

Arrived at the house of his prey, the flying *asuwáng* perches on the roof and lets out his long thread-like tongue. This passes through the nipa shingles and is made to contact the sick person lying below. Since the tongue is hollow, the *asuwáng* can draw up the blood or phlegm he seeks. His night's work over, the *asuwáng* returns home to feed his family. The *anananggál* drops his internal organs into the waiting trunk, puts his head in the proper position, and is once more intact. Some informants say that a bath in the river is sufficient to remove the ill-smelling ointment and its concomitant powers, while others would add a formula, very brief in form, which is translated "There *is* a God at night." This profession undoes the pact with the evil spirits and restores the *asuwáng* to his former state. He is back at his home with the first streaks of .dawn in the east.

Flying *asuwáng* are associated, more often than walking *asuwáng,* with the disturbance of the newly buried. They are said to fly to the cemetery and there feed themselves on the corpses of recent arrivals. They may even take a body home for the family, usually changing the human appearance to that of a pig, lest anyone be indisposed to eat of the food.

The capturing of lone travelers is another feat of the flying *asuwáng.* They are said to swoop down between the legs of their prey and carry them aloft, usually drowning them in a carabao wallow before devouring them. This action is usually taken by *female asuwáng* (most flying *asuwáng* are female) who have been spurned in love. In vengeance they seize the ungrateful male and do away with him.

Becoming an asuwáng: *prerequisites.* Negatively, it is already clear that sex is no barrier for one desiring to be an *asuwáng.* Both males and females are said to belong to this class of human beings. There is no set age at which one may become an *asuwáng,* for there are said to be entire families of this nature. However, the active members of these groups are always fully matured men and women. There seem to be *no* special *physical* requirements.

The important prerequisites are all of a *moral* nature. The prospective *asuwáng* must be a person with little or no faith in God, and less in his fellow men. He must be a secretive, asocial, misanthropic creature who dislikes normal concourse with men and despises the things of God and of the church. Usually, persons of little or no educational attainment are best suited to be *asuwáng,* but we are told that very literate and talented persons have become *asuwáng.* To summarize, the would-be *asuwáng* should be a person at odds with God and men, friendly only with evil spirits and fellow *asuwáng.*

Becoming an asuwáng: *processes.* There are four principal ways in which one may become an *asuwáng;* namely, by personal effort, by transmission, by contamination, by heredity.

In becoming an *asuwáng* by one's personal effort, one need not have the cooperation of another who is already an *asuwáng.* A fertilized chicken egg is held "against the stomach"; then it is bound in place by means of a cloth which is wrapped around the body. After a period of time unspecified in length, the *chick* passes into the stomach by a process of osmosis. At this time the operator will be able to emit the sound characteristic of the true *asuwáng;* he will be able to cry *kakák* or *kikík.* The egg shell is not thrown away; it is placed in a bamboo tube in the mixture of coconut oil and chicken dung which was spoken of above.

Another way to acquire the power and nature of an *asuwáng* independently is the following. After the procession of Good Friday, the aspirant proceeds to the cemetery, carrying two fertilized chicken eggs.

This must be done at night. Standing erect, gazing directly at the full moon without winking, the candidate places one egg under each armpit. He mumbles the required words — unfortunately not known to the informants — three times. With the disappearance of the *eggs,* we are told, the man has become an *asuwáng.* The same procedure is followed in the *asuwáng's* yearly *renewal* of power.

The process of becoming an *asuwáng* by *transmission* is similar to the first method in that the procedure is usually voluntary, but it differs in that the cooperation of a true *asuwáng* is required. This process and that of contamination, to be explained below, are the methods most commonly mentioned by informants.

The form of transmission spoken of by almost all informants is the transfer of power made by a dying *asuwáng.* It is a widespread belief that an *asuwáng* simply refuses to die until someone in the family circle, or some friend, will accept the *antíng-antíng* ("charm"; in this case the chick within the *asuwáng)* and the power which accompanies it. When the obliging person has stepped forward, he bends low over the expiring *asuwáng,* till their mouths are only one or two inches apart. The *asuwáng's* chick then hops out of its former host's mouth and into that of the new *asuwáng.* When the weakening *asuwáng* sees his successor wallow hard, he passes away, content.

Some informants mention this same process as being used when the *asuwáng* is in perfectly good health but wishes to transfer his powers to another. The veteran and the candidate overlap their tongues and the chick hops across the bridge and down into the stomach of the new *asuwáng*.

Another method of transmission is the culmination of a course of instruction given by an *asuwáng* to a person who has asked to be taught the secrets of the profession. The act whereby the candidate becomes a true member of the inner circle is the eating of a morsel of human flesh prepared by the veteran *asuwáng*.

The process of *contamination* is known to all informants, probably because all feel in imminent danger of having some *asuwáng* use this method to their ruin. The *asuwáng* need only drop some of his saliva, or a piece of human flesh into the food of the unsuspecting victim and the harm is done. (In Appendix 1 will be found the story of a man whose wife had been so contaminated by a spurned lover.)

One informant gives an elaborate form of contamination. The *asuwáng* places a hair, pulled from his own head, between his teeth; one end of the hair is placed in the mouth of another person — without that person's knowledge or consent, in sleep. When the *asuwáng's* saliva crosses the hair-bridge and enters the mouth of the sleeping victim, the latter becomes an *asuwáng*.

Only one investigator, reporting from Iriga, Camarines Sur, mentions the method of *heredity*. He was told by two informants that the *asuwáng* nature is passed on by simple heredity for *seven* generations. The very fact that a child is born of an *asuwáng* is, in this case, sufficient to make that child an *asuwáng*. It will not be out of place to mention here that the town of Iriga is perhaps the most interesting town, from many viewpoints, in the entire Bicol region. It is traditionally considered a special center for *asuwáng*. The very mention of the name "Iriga" is sufficient to evoke from high school or college students the reply, "That's where there are many *asuwáng*." The people of Iriga have more centralized ideas about the location of the *asuwáng* habitats, usually fixing upon one of the outlying barrios, such as Mabonga. The association of Iriga with *asuwáng* may be accounted for, in part at least, by the fact that on the slopes of Mt. Iriga, which overlooks the town, there live about two thousand *Agtâ*, semi- Negroid hill people.[9]

Characteristics of asuwáng: *physical appearance.* In general, it is said that *by day* the *asuwáng* look tired, pale, thin — because of their lack or proper sleep. Some informants maintain that they are also stoop-shouldered, a characteristic acquired by their continually going under the houses of the sick. *By night,* the *asuwáng* present a different appearance, for then they are strong, vigorous and active. It is said that both male and female dress in the ordinary

---

[9] The Mt. Iriga *Agtâ* are a semi-nomadic people most of whom are engaged as *abaká*-strippers. For a short description of this group, see the the author's "Some Notes on a Brief Field Survey of the Hill People of Mt. Iriga, Camarines Sur, Philippines," *Primitive Man* 21 (1948) 65-73.

manner during the day, but that the female, despite her fatigue, seems exceptionally beautiful. Her hair is usually very long and it is this hair, according to some, which becomes stiff at night and helps to propel the flying female *asuwáng*. (Minor details of the physical appearance of *asuwáng* will be noted in a subsequent section dealing with the detection of *asuwáng*.)

Characteristics of asuwáng: *physical powers.* In the discussion of various kinds of *asuwáng,* earlier in this paper, most of their preternatural abilities were described. Here they are merely summarized, with a few minor additions.

The *asuwáng* have, first of all, the power of flight and/or swift, elusive walking. They have the power to transform themselves into any object, animate or inanimate, and to render themselves and other things invisible. They can, at will, change the form of persons or things to suit their convenience. Their perception is intensely keen, especially in hearing and seeing. Their strength at night is immense: the female *asuwáng* is said to have the strength of ten able-bodied men. With their saliva they can xxxx any wound which has been inflicted on them.

Characteristics of asuwáng: *likes and dislikes.* By day the *asuwáng* shun the normal informal social gatherings held in the neighborhood, such as the women's group at the river, come together for washing, bathing and exchanging small-talk, or the men's usual gathering at some favorite store or barbershop. They seek solitude and are given a wide berth by all. By night the *asuwáng* shun all light except that of the moon, and are said to be happiest when the moon is "just beginning to round." They have an avid appetite for the blood, phlegm, mucus and even odors of the tubercular sick; they enjoy the flesh and blood of the newly dead, especially infants. On the other hand, they detest any kind of lemon or garlic, and cannot bear the odor of certain other foods and plants to be mentioned in a subsequent section of this paper.

Restoration of asuwáng *to normal human state.* There are two distinct kinds of restoration known to most of the informants: the *temporary* restoration effected by the *asuwáng* himself at the end of a night's operations, and the *permanent* restoration, normally brought about by persons other than the *asuwáng.*

Temporary recovery may be accomplished in one of several ways, some of which have been explained in an earlier section of this paper. The mere satisfaction of his appetite is sufficient, according to some, to restore the *asuwáng,* with the coming of dawn, to the state of a normal human. Others say that it is entirely in the will, and that the *asuwáng's* transformation is as simple as "taking off one's coat." Most informants, however, maintain that a bath in the river is necessary to remove the magical ointment and its powers. It is for this reason that many old men speak of early morning bathing as a very bad sign.

Permanent restoration is a more drastic operation. Informants are unanimous, or almost unanimous, in the belief that there is only one permanent cure for an *asuwáng:* the chick must be gotten from its hiding place in the *asuwáng's* stomach, and be destroyed. This removal may be, effected in one of two ways. The *asuwáng* may be strung up by the heels, head downward, and the chick brought out of the *asuwáng's* mouth by means of a prolonged beating of the hanging *asuwáng's* back and stomach, or by means of a sickening spinning of his body. A fire is built under the *asuwáng*, many informants tell us, and this fire speeds up the sickening process. The same fire will destroy the vomited chick (one informant substitutes several caldrons of boiling water for the same purpose). A relatively more considerate method of permanent cure is described in Appendix I. In this process, the *asuwáng* is seated in a suspended chair and the chair is spun till the patient vomits the chick. As in the first method, however, the chick is immediately destroyed by fire, lest it hop back into the cured person's mouth.

Measures taken against asuwáng: *detection.* Many and varied are the means by which one can know that a suspected person is really an *asuwáng*. Most of these tests are for daytime diagnoses, but several informants have revealed ways of detecting the presence of an *asuwáng* when he is about his nightly business.

There are two criteria which are almost universally known. If the suspected party, when speaking to the person who suspects him, does not look him squarely in the face, but shifts his gaze restlessly and guiltily, the suspect is indeed an *asuwáng*. This diagnosis can be confirmed if the investigator is able to get a good look at the suspect's eyes; for if the *taó-taó* ("pseudoman"; the reflection of the investigator seen in the suspect's eyes) is *upside-down,* there can be no doubt that the person is an *asuwáng*.

Some informants say that if a leaf of the *talampúnay* plant (*Datura metel* Linn.) is rubbed on the palm of an *asuwáng,* or seeds of the same plant put on his head, he will automatically cry *kakák*. The same effect may be produced by soundly punching the *asuwáng's* middle. One informant says that the toes of an *asuwáng* always point upward; another tolls us that the usual notch between the bottom of the nose and the upper lip (the philtrum) is missing, and its place is a smooth, unridged skin surface. Still another informant claims that an *asuwáng* can be detected by his behavior in church, during the Mass. When the priest turns to bless the congregation, the *asuwáng* will be seen trying to "dodge" the blessing.

There are several ways of detecting the presence of an *asuwáng* at night. The cry of *kakák* and *kikík* has already been mentioned. A scratching on the roof is at least a caution signal, for if it is not a roosting hen, it is an *asuwáng*. If a baby cries for no apparent reason, or if a sick person suddenly becomes uneasy, or if the atmosphere turns warm and fetid abruptly, there is an *asuwáng* about. A dog, pig or cat with no tail is very probably an *asuwáng* in disguise.

Measures taken against asuwáng: *prevention from doing harm.* It is especially in the preventive measures used against *asuwáng* that we note many practices connected with Christianity. The attacks of *asuwáng* are discouraged by the use of holy water, blessed palms (from Palm Sunday), incense, and the displaying of the crucifix.[10]

The use of the *oración* deserves special mention. Nominally, it is a prayer; in reality, it is a garbled collection of Latin words and phrases, copied from a missal or from inscriptions seen in the church. The meaningless phrase *Dominus spiritu cum vobiscum fratres tuo* is typical. The *oración* is written down on a slip of paper or in a little book and carried as a powerful weapon against the *asuwáng* and the evil spirits. Whether the users of the *oración* regard it as something more than a magical formula is difficult to say. At any rate, the *oración,* if recited in or under the house of a sick person, is believed to ward off the attacks of the *asuwáng.*

So much for preventive measures connected with Christianity. Besides these, there are various fruits, spices, seeds, leaves, woods and whole plants which are thought to be efficacious against *asuwáng.*

---

[10] It is easy to understand why many informants should recommend the use of holy water against the *asuwáng.* They believe that *asuwáng* are under the influence of the evil spirits. Likewise, they know that one of the reasons for which the priest blesses holy water is that it might be used in dispelling the power of the evil spirit.

Most commonly mentioned by informants is the lemon (*lemonsíto. kalamansî,* etc.), which may be used in various ways. If one must walk alone at night along a deserted path or road, he should either carry some slices of the *lemonsíto* or rub his body thoroughly with the juice. This will keep the *asuwáng* at a distance, for they detest the small of the lemon. If a sick person is to be protected, a few slices (some specify three) should be placed under his mat or bed. *Báwang* (garlic, *Allium sativum* Linn.) may be used in the same manner.

The *talampúnay* plant (*Datura metel* Linn.) has been noted in connection with the discovery of a person who is suspected to be an *asuwáng*. The seeds of this plant provide a means to discourage the approach of *asuwáng*. Scattered about on the ground, under and around the house, these seeds will keep the *asuwáng* at bay. Moreover, the burning of *talampúnay* leaves or the growing of the plant near the house has the same salutary effect. Similarly, the leaves of the *gábi-gábi* (*Bootia renifolia* Merr.) may be burned, as may certain unspecified tree woods and leaves, the burning of which produces a pungent odor.

The snout of a sawfish and the tail of a sting-ray are mentioned by several informants. The latter is either displayed in the house or used to "whip the houseposts" under the structure.

The burning of chicken feathers, rubber, leather and other materials which produce a strong and disagreeable odor will discourage the *asuwáng*. Fish hooks hung under the house floor, or sharp *bolo* blades suspended, point downward through the floor, are also effective.

A very important preventive means, frequently noted by the investigators, is the lighting of the interior and underside of the house. Moreover, it is well to keep the window openings tightly closed.

One specific measure, which is adopted against the possibility of capture at night by a flying *asuwáng,* is indicated by several informants. It will be remembered that the flying *asuwáng* is wont to seize upon lone travelers by swooping between the legs of the victim and carrying him off. The traveler, when he suspects that an *asuwáng* is about to attack, should throw himself flat upon the ground until the danger has passed.

Measures taken against asuwáng: *capture.* By far the majority of methods for capturing *asuwáng* depend upon distraction or the use of a decoy for their effectiveness. There are mentioned only a few processes which cannot be reduced to these categories.

The basic principle of the process of distraction is to provide the *asuwáng* with some diverting activity which will so occupy his attention that he will not only forget the reason for which he came to the sick person's house, but also be easy to capture by surprise.

The trap is prepared in very simple fashion. Seeds are scattered about under the house either by dropping them through the split-bamboo floor, or by scattering them broadcast while standing under the house. If the latter procedure is used, informants usually insist that the person scattering the seeds should allow no light to shine on himself, for this would make it impossible for him to see the *asuwáng* in the dark. The seeds most commonly suggested are those of the *talampúnay,* but rice, mustard-seed and corn are also permitted.

Armed with a *cordón* (the cincture worn by the priest at Mass), the *asuwáng*-hunter takes his place in the shadows of the house. When the *asuwáng* (ordinarily the walking species) arrives, he will notice the seeds and will at once begin to pick them up one by one. He *will* not and *cannot* interrupt his task till every single seed, grain or kernel has been retrieved. When the lurking hunter is certain that the *asuwáng* is totally absorbed in this activity, he must dash from his hiding place and cast the *cordón* aroung the *asuwáng's* body. The *asuwáng* is then powerless and must submit to the curative treatment described earlier in this paper.

The *cordón* is not always used. Sometimes a *bolo* is employed, but this method can easily fail; for if the *asuwáng* is not struck in the middle of the back, he may be able to apply some of his saliva to the wound and thus cure himself. However, if the attacker lands the prescribed blow, the capture or death of the *asuwáng* is assured. Even though the *asuwáng* should manage to get away that night, he will be found in his house the next day, bleeding, dying or dead.

In the *decoy* method of capture, the *cordón* or *bolo* is again employed. Armed with either of these weapons, the decoy waits under the house of the sick person. He must be sure no light fails on himself. As the *asuwáng* approaches, the hunter must — in typical *asuwáng* fashion — hang from the house joists directly beneath the sick person. The real *asuwáng,* seeing this other *"asuwáng"* enjoying himself so, will beg a share. With a great show of reluctance, the pseudo- *asuwáng* yields his place to the newcomer. Once the real *asuwáng* has turned his attention to the sick person, it is easy for the pseudo-*asuwáng,* standing beside him, to bring *bolo* or *cordón* into play as in the distraction process.

There are several more direct methods of capture mentioned by two or three informants. One such process consists in lying in wait for the *asuwáng* and pouncing upon him, effecting final capture by use of the *cordón,* the *bolo* or — if there are many attackers — sheer brawn. One informant says that to catch the *asuwáng* one must place three "two-eyed" coconut shell on the ground under the house of the sick; seated on these, the attacker is invisible to the *asuwáng* and can easily surprise and overpower him when he appears. Another informant claims that it is only necessary to hide in the shadows near the house and to begin the recitation of an *oración* when the *asuwáng* arrives; the *asuwáng* is made powerless.

How can one detect *and capture* an *asuwáng* during

the day? Two investigators have reported slightly different methods, but both are concerned with the apprehension of suspected visitors in one's house. If a guest is thought to be an *asuwáng,* the test is simple. A *needle,* stuck into the door jamb, will tell the story: if the visitor, when about to leave, approaches the door but cannot pass through the opening, he is an *asuwáng.* Capture is easy, since by day the *asuwáng* have normal or sub-normal strength. The other method makes use of a *sig-hid,* the common type of short, unhalted broom.[11] This broom, if placed in an inverted position near the door, will have the same effect as the needle in the preceding process.

A special method, to be used for the capture of an *asuwáng na layóg* or flying *asuwáng,* is reported by Ramon Brillante from the town of Camaligan, near Naga, Camarines Sur. It contains an interesting mixture of simple imitative magic with Christian accretions. It is here quoted in full from the investigator's report.

"In the case of the *asuwáng na layóg,* the old man had this to say: 'Prepare three big stones (a stove) and three big nails. The moment you hear the familiar *"Kakák! Kakák!"* begin to recite the *Minatúhod* (Apostles' Creed). When you reach that part which

---

[11] "The *sig-hid* is made from coconut-paint fronds. A bunch of the dried mid-ribs arc bound together at, one end to form a broom about (two and one-half feet long and about one foot wide at the unbound end. Some informants say that *asuwáng* frequently hide behind the *sig-hid;* to prevent this, tin broom should be inverted (stood on its bound end).

says *"ipináko sa kurús"* ("was crucified"; literally, "was *nailed* to the cross"), pick up one of the stones and drive one of the nails into the ground. Go through the entire process twice more. You will then notice that the flying *asuwáng,* regardless of how far he has down from you, will turn back and perch himself on the three stove-like stones. Nor it was there that you *nailed* him in the prayer."

Functions of the asuwáng *belief.* There are at least two outstanding offices performed by this belief: it helps in the management of children and acts as an impelling motive for adults to strive for social conduct in their community. The first function is easily explained by saying that the *asuwáng* is for many Bicol mothers what the "bogey man" is for many American mothers. A child's crying can be stopped instantly by the warning, "If you don't stop that crying, the *asuwáng* will come and get you." A child will lose his interest in afterdark wanderings if he is reminded that the *asuwáng* are abroad and looking for the likes of him. In many such ways the belief is used to discipline children.

The social function in the life of adults can be understood by a consideration of two elements of the *asuwáng* belief; namely, the characteristics by which an *asuwáng* may be recognized, and the combined fear, distrust and scorn which is directed toward proven or even suspected *asuwáng.* No normal person wishes to be suspected of being an *asuwáng.* The result is that he sedulously tries to avoid showing any of the traits of the *asuwáng.* such as secretiveness, solitariness, misanthropy and the like. In this manner the belief discourages any asocial attitudes.

Since the *asuwáng* tradition is an almost universal belief or near-belief, a subsidiary function appears.
A knowledge of the nature of *asuwáng,* and a store of tales about their activities — especially when personal encounters are involved — are a source of *prestige* among young and old alike.

Conclusion. In keeping with the purpose of the present paper, the propositions derived from this study are of a descriptive nature. No attempt is made to compare the Bicol belief with similar beliefs in other parts of the Philippines, nor is the Bicol belief itself subjected to an analysis which would test the objective validity of any of its elements. The conclusions which follow are valid in a general manner, for the provinces of Camarines Sur and Albay.

(1) The *asuwáng* belief is living and functional.

(2) This belief contains in itself many elements of imitative magic as well as certain ideas derived from Christianity.

(3) An *asuwáng,* according to this belief, is a man or woman possessing preternatural powers of locomotion and metamorphosis, and an inhuman appetite for the voided phlegm and sputum of the

deathly sick, as well as the flesh and blood of the newly dead. These powers and appetites are acquired either by a pact, implicit or explicit, with the evil spirits, or by means of imitative magic, or both.

APPENDIX I

Quoted here in full is the story of an informant's personal dealings with an *asuwáng,* his deceased wife. The narrative was recorded by Vivencio Belga in the town of Magarao, xxxxx Sur.

"It was towards the close of the nineteenth century, while I was a *sacristán* of the parish priest of [a Bicol town], that I was attracted by a beautiful woman (my deceased wife) who used to visit the church. This woman had the bad reputation of being an *asuwáng.* Yet, in spite of her ill repute, I was decided to win her.

"When I proposed to her, she was honest enough to admit that she was 'feeling something' which had begun shortly after she had rejected a former suitor. She told me that at times, during the night, she felt an irresistible desire to go under the houses of the sick and to swallow the sputum of sick persons. She said that her father had ordered the former suitor (an *asuwáng,* whom she had rejected) to cook their food. He was seen by one of their immediate neighbors putting some of his saliva, together with something like powder, into her food. This, she believed, had made her an *asuwáng.*

"I wished she had not related her story to me, for I became greatly worried. I lost no time, however, in remedying the situation. I asked everyone whom I knew how I could cure her. Finally I was advised that the best remedy was to tie her in a chair and, by means of a rope tied to the chair, elevate her from the ground and spin her round and round. This I suggested to her and she readily consented.

"After turning her round and round for half an hour, she vomited a yellowish watery substance; after another fifteen minutes, she vomited another watery substance, this time whitish and very sticky. I was nearly overcome with pity by her entreaties to stop; she was very weak by now and complained at being turned round again. But I was determined to follow my instructions and thus cure her. I had been told to continue the spinning for three hours.

"I turned her round and round once more, until there was little life left in her. I was about to stop spinning her when she vomited a little yellow chick, with its feathers just beginning to grow. I tried to catch the chick, but it was very quick in hopping and showed efforts to reach my sweetheart's mouth again. Since it had no wings as yet, the only thing it could do was hop and jump in the direction of her mouth. Finally I succeeded in catching it and immediately placed it in the fire. After this the spell of the *asuwáng* went away from my sweetheart and she was cured."

To this account the investigator added the note: "The informant further commented that if the chick had been given sufficient time to grow its wings in the body of his sweetheart, she would have been able to fly."

APPENDIX II

Given here is the local distribution of reports submitted in April 1948 by students of the Ateneo de Naga college department, whom the author had trained as investigators in the *asuwáng* belief.

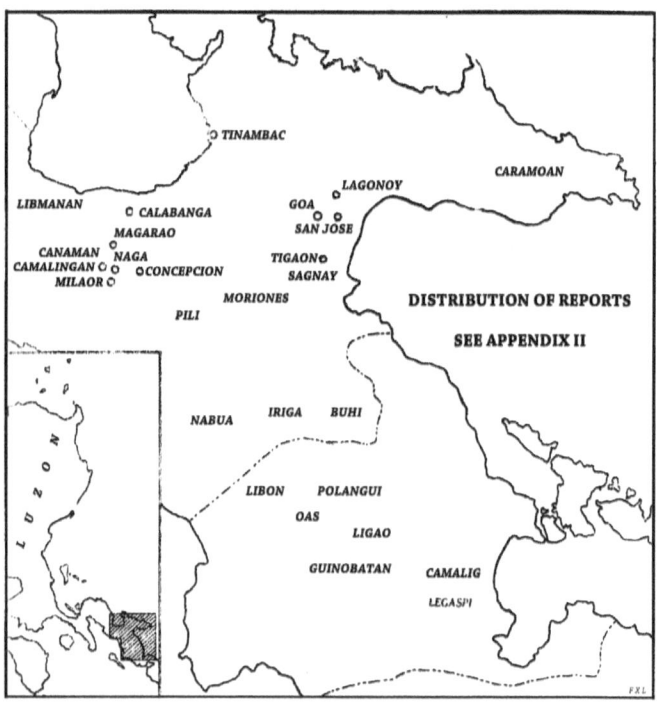

Camarines Sur (20 towns; 46 reports; 88 informants)

A. *Caramoan Peninsula* (1 town; 2 reports; 2 informants)

1. Caramoan (2 reports; 2 informants)

B. *Partido de Lagonoy* (5 town; 7 reports; 18 informants)

2. Lagonoy (1 report; 3 informants)

3. Goa (1 report; 3 informants)

4. San Jose (1 report; 2 informants)

5. Tigaon (1 report; 2 informants)

6. Sagnay (3 reports; 8 informants)

C. *Naga district* (6 towns; 18 reports; 38 informants)

7. Naga (8 reports; 16 informants)

8. Canaman (1 report; 1 informant)

9. Camaligan (4 reports; 5 informants)

10. Concepcion (1 report; 3 informants)

11. Milaor (1 report; 1 informant)

12. Magarao (3 reports; 12 informants)

D.   *San Miguel district* (3 towns; 4 reports; 3 informants)

13.   Calabanga (2 reports; 3 informants)

14.   Tinambac (1 report; 1 informant)

15.   Libmanan (1 report; 1 informant)

E.   *Pili-Rinconada district* (5 towns; 15 reports; 25 informants)

16.   Pili (2 reports; 3 informants)

17.   Moriones (1 report; 3 informants)

18.   Buhi (1 report; 1 informant)

19.   Iriga (6 reports; 12 informants)

20.   Nabua (5 reports; 7 informants)

Albay (7 towns; 11 reports; 29 informants)

21.   Libon (1 report; 4 informants)

22.   Polangui (1 report; 1 informant)

23.   Oas (2 reports; 8 informants)

24.   Ligao (1 report; 1 informant)

25.   Guinobatan (1 report; 2 informants)

26.   Camalig (1 report; 3 informants)

27.   Legaspi (4 reports; 10 informants)

Total: 27 towns; 57 reports; 117 informants.

The informants were almost evenly divided into male and female, with age-range limits of 35 and 90. The average age was approximately 60 years.

The author's personal notes were derived for the most part from younger informant, 15 to 25 years old, the majority male.

APPENDIX III

According to Castaño's *Noticia del Bicol,* there was an *asuwáng* tradition in the Bicol region when, toward the end of the sixteenth century, the first missionaries began to labor there. Quoted here are pertinent selections from the work of Fr. Castaño.[1]

"They [the Bicolanos at the arrival of the Spanish missionaries] believed that *Gugurang* was the *good God,* the beneficent spirit of their region, the defender and guardian of their homes, who protected their interests from the malice of *Asuang.* The latter, on the other hand, was the evil spirit, the sovereign rival of *Gugurang,* a spirit malicious by nature, whose sole pleasure lay in doing them what harm he could. *Gugurang,* they though, always lent a propitious ear to their prayers and granted whatever they asked, whether this was some good for themselves or some vengeance on their enemies; and they looked upon him with the greatest good will and respect. But they always cursed *Asuang,* since from him they expected countless evils; and, obsessed by the idea that he could do them harm, they fled in fear and excitement, not knowing where to hide. The very thought of *Asuang* so tormented them that when it flashed across

---

[1] The full title of the *Noticia* is "Breve Noticia acerca del Origen, Religion, Crecncias, y Supersticiones dc los antiguos Indios del Bícol" por el P. Fr. José Castaño. Madrid, 1895. Pages 57. In *Archivo del Bibliófilo Filipino* (Madrid: Casa de la Viuda de M. Minuesa de los Rios, 1895) Vol. 1. The translation used here is by Jaime C. Bulatao, S. J. For Bicol words, Castaño's orthography is retained.

their minds they would abandon what they were doing, and would at times be heard crying out piteously in their uncontrollable fear, uttering horrible maledictions and sighing aloud. Above all did mothers with little children try at all cost to keep them carefully hidden, in fear lest *Asuang* drain their blood and steal their entrails." (pages 21-22)

"Moreover, they had a superstitious belief in the existence of Bonggos, evil and perverse spirits, servants of *Asuang,* who wandered by his orders through the forest thicknesses. The *Bonggós* were beings human in shape, black and very ugly. Whenever they appeared, they shot from their eyes flaming sparks to consume whomsoever they chose of those within range. They were the fiercest of the menials of *Asuang*, and preceded him in his raids of vengeance; these latter took place whenever the *Corócoó,* the night bird, uttered its dark and mournful cry. This cry was, in the minds of the people, a certain sign that *Asuang* was approaching and about to devour the entrails of a child. Hence it was that they tried with all anxiety and diligence to hide their children from the sight of all, and to guard them carefully till the mournful cry of the *Corócoó* had died upon the night. But if then they heard a dull sound like the rumbling of a distant storm, at once were they tilled with a terrible fear and unreasoning trembling; for they believed that *Asuang* had actually come and was carrying off the entrails of some child or of some sick person, and that soon someone of the *dulujan* would have to die.

"They believed in the existence of *Irago* or, as others called it, *Oriol,* a fabulous serpent, daughter of *Asuang,* which disappeared immediately after it had appeared to the sight of men. Its mission was to seduce the person it was bewitching and to draw him where it wished. It led people on to concubinage, robbery, revenge; and they could resist neither its attracting nor its urging. About this serpent they told many a tale and gave all kinds of foolish advice, as one would expect from the savage state in which they lived.

"They also looked upon *Yasáo* as an evil spirit, and had for him great fear and respect. He was some horrible kind of phantom that appeared on moonlit nights in the shade of the trees, and delighted in scaring them and filling them with trembling fear. If at his appearance they heard or seemed to hear cries, certain it was that one of them was about to die, for *Asuang* was coming to make the *lalahan*, the kill. This *Yasáo* changed himself at times into a *Laqui*, a monster with the hoofs and skin of a goat and the face of a very ugly man. In this shape he wandered through the forest, thus punished by *Asuang* for his indolence in tormenting men, but daring to hurt no man." (pages 23-25)

"The worship of *Asuang* was very common and widespread, almost as much as that of *Gugnrang.* This worship, in consonance with the beliefs they held of him, was for the most part expiatory; for since they considered him the spirit of evil and the efficient cause of every injury and harm they suffered, it is not surprising that they tried to placate him, using all the means within their limited power, even the savage and barbaric shedding of human blood. The worship given *Asuang* differed according to the reasons which prompted it.

"The *Hidhid* was a kind of execration or exorcism. Whenever public calamity befell the region, such as locust-plague, pests or destructive typhoon, the *baliana* performed the *Hidhid* over that region, vehemently blaming *Asuang* and even ordering him with authority to withdraw from and abandon that land. When the *baliana* performed the *Hidhid* over some sick person who had come under the influence of the spirit of *Asuang,* she would be in by placing on the patient's head xxxx poultice of ground and kneaded xxxx leaves (the powerful, efficacious and universal medicine of the xxxx for all their ailments); then, keeping it there, she would make several turns around the patient, dancing and twisting countless times, gesturing and praying, while she conjured *Asuang* to leave. If the patient was cured, they said that the cure was due to the efficacy of her exorcism; but if he died, his death was due to the fact that *Asuang*, the evil *Asuang,* wished to bring him to *Gagamban*, there to suffer with him horrible tortures." (pages 33-34)

"It anyone had a son whom he deeply loved — and in this matter of filial affection they (especially the women) go to extremes — he would, to free his son from the curse of *Asuang*, perform with him the xxxx, that is, the sacred offering made to the *Anitos* of their ancestors. To do this, they take the boy up in their arms and, very quickly, carry him from one side of the house to the other, that *Asuang* might go away and the son be free, under the protection and patronage of his *Anitos.* " (page 38)

About The Author

Frank Lynch was born on April 2, 1921 at Orange, New Jersey, U.S.A. He received his earlier education from Fordham Preparatory and Fordham College in New York, N.Y., and Woodstock College in Maryland. In 1949, he received his M.A. in anthropology from the University of the Philippines. Later he went to the University of Chicago to earn his Ph.D. in anthropology in 1959.

Father Lynch specialized in the field of social anthropology and is well-known for his studies on Philippine values. He had written about one hundred and fifty essays, articles, monographs and books on the Philippines and the Filipino people.

At the time of his death, Father Lynch was resident consultant of the Institute of Philippine Culture, Ateneo de Manila University, professor of anthropology and chairman of the Department of Anthropology, Ateneo, and director of the Social Survey Research Unit, Ateneo de Naga. He also served as consultant of the Project Development Division of the Population Center Foundation. He was also the discipline representative for anthropology to the PSSC Executive Board. (Source: PSSC Social Science Information, 1978)

www.ingramcontent.com/pod-product-compliance
Lightning Source LLC
Chambersburg PA
CBHW020331290526
45785CB00007B/3009